LifeChange

A NAVPRESS BIBLE STUDY SERIES

A life-changing
encounter with God's Word

PARABLES OF GRACE

Jesus' stories invite us to experience
the loving-kindness of God.

Published in alliance with Tyndale House Publishers

CONTENTS

HOW TO USE THIS STUDY

Objectives

The topical guides in the LifeChange series of Bible studies cover important topics from the Bible. Although the LifeChange guides vary with the topics they explore, they share some common goals:

1. to help readers grasp what key passages in the Bible say about the topic;

2. to provide readers with explanatory notes, word definitions, historical background, and cross-references so that the only other reference they need is the Bible;

3. to teach readers how to let God's Word transform them into Christ's image;

4. to provide small groups with a tool that will enhance group discussion of each passage and topic; and

5. to write each session so that advance preparation for group members is strongly encouraged but not required.

Each lesson in this study is designed to take forty-five minutes to complete.

Overview and Details

The study begins with an overview of Jesus' parables about grace. The key to interpretation for each part of this study is content (what is the referenced passage *about*?), and the key to context is purpose (what is the author's *aim* for the passage as it relates to the overall topic?). The individual lessons of the study explore what these parables show us about grace with corresponding passages from the Bible.

Kinds of Questions

Bible study provides different lenses and perspectives through which to engage the Scripture: observe (what does the passage *say*?), interpret (what does the passage *mean*?), and apply (how does this truth *affect* my life?). Some of the "how" and "why" questions will take some creative thinking, even prayer, to answer. Some are opinion questions without clear-cut right answers; these will lend themselves to discussions and side studies.

Don't let your study become an exercise in knowledge alone. Treat the passage as God's Word, and stay in dialogue with Him as you study. Pray, *Lord, what do You want me to see here?*, *Father, why is this true?*, and *Lord, how does this apply to my life?*

It is important that you write down your answers. The act of writing clarifies your thinking and helps you remember what you're learning.

Study Aids

Throughout the guide, there are study aids that provide background information on the passage, insights from commentaries, and word studies. These aids are included in the guide to help you interpret the Bible without needing to use outside resources. Still, if you're interested in exploring further, the full resources are listed in the endnotes.

Scripture Versions

Unless otherwise indicated, the Bible quotations in this guide are from the New International Version of the Bible. The other version cited is the English Standard Version.

Use any translation you like for study—or preferably more than one. Ideally you would have on hand a good modern translation such as the New International Version, the English Standard Version, the New Living Translation, or the Christian Standard Bible. A paraphrase such as *The Message* is not accurate enough for study, but it can be helpful for comparison or devotional reading.

Memorizing and Meditating

A psalmist wrote, "I have hidden your word in my heart that I might not sin against you" (Psalm 119:11). If you write down a verse or passage that challenges or encourages you and reflect on it often for a week or more, you will find it beginning to affect your motives and actions. We forget quickly what we read once; we remember what we ponder.

When you find a significant verse or passage, you might copy it onto a card to keep with you. Set aside five minutes each day just to think about what the passage might mean in your life. Recite it to yourself, exploring its meaning. Then, return to the passage as often as you can during the day for a brief review. You will soon find it coming to mind spontaneously.

For Group Study

A group of four to ten people allows for the richest discussions, but you can adapt this guide for other-sized groups. It will suit a wide range of group types, such as home Bible studies, growth groups, youth groups, and workplace Bible studies. Both new and experienced Bible students, and new and mature Christians, will benefit from the guide. You can omit or leave for later any questions you find too easy or too hard.

The guide is intended to lead a group through one lesson per meeting. This guide is formatted so you will be able to discuss each of the questions at length. Be sure to make time at each discussion for members to ask about anything they didn't understand.

Each member should prepare for a meeting by writing answers for all the background and discussion questions to be covered. Application will be very difficult, however, without private thought and prayer.

Two reasons for studying in a group are accountability and support. When each member commits in front of the rest to seek growth in an area of life, you can pray for one another, listen jointly for God's guidance, help one another resist temptation, assure each other that each person's growth matters to you, use the group to practice spiritual principles, and so on. Pray about one another's commitments and needs at most meetings. If you wish, you can spend the first few minutes of each meeting sharing any results from applications prompted by previous lessons and discuss new applications toward the end of the meeting. Follow your time of sharing with prayer for these and other needs.

If you write down what others have shared, you are more likely to remember to pray for them during the week, ask about what they shared at the next meeting, and notice answered prayers. You might want to get a notebook for prayer requests and discussion notes.

Taking notes during discussion will help you remember to follow up on ideas, stay on the subject, and have clarity on an issue. But don't let note-taking keep you from participating.

Some best practices for groups:

1. If possible, come to the group discussion prepared. The more each group member knows about the passage and the questions being asked, the better your discussion will be.

2. Realize that the group leader will not be teaching from the passage but instead will be facilitating your discussion. Therefore, it is important for each group member to participate so that everyone can contribute to what you learn as a group.

3. Try to stick to the passage covered in the session and the specific questions in the study guide.

4. Listen attentively to the other members of the group when they are sharing their thoughts about the passage. Also realize that most of the questions are open-ended, allowing for more than one answer.

5. Be careful not to dominate the discussion—especially if you are the leader. Allow time for everyone to share their thoughts and ideas.

6. As mentioned previously, throughout the session are study aids that provide background information on the passage, insights from commentaries, and word studies. Reading these aloud during the meeting is optional and up to the discussion leader. However, each member can refer to these insights if they found them helpful in understanding the passage.

A Note on Topical Studies

LifeChange guides offer robust and thoughtful engagement with God's Word. The book-centric guides focus on a step-by-step walk through that particular book of the Bible. The topical studies use Scripture to help you engage more deeply with God's Word and its implications for your life.

INTRODUCTION

The Parables of Jesus

DURING HIS TIME ON EARTH, Jesus did not develop a step-by-step discipleship program or generally preach long sermons. Rather, He preferred to meet people right where they were, explaining ideas through vivid and relevant short stories. These illustrations connected to life in first-century Palestine, drawing from nature, dinner parties, the rich and the poor, and family relationships. The name of this teaching tool? Parables. New Testament scholar Arland J. Hultgren explains, "A parable is a figure of speech in which a comparison is made between God's kingdom, actions, or expectations and something in this world, real or imagined."[1]

We can easily treat these familiar stories as simple lessons with moral takeaways, but then we risk missing who Jesus is and what He came to do. As we unpack the historical context and hear the parables as Jesus' first followers would have heard them, we will find that these parables are radical, shocking, and challenging—not only for the original listeners but also for us today.

Throughout this study, we will pay special attention to what the parables reveal about God's character, God's Kingdom, and God's grace. The main Greek word for "grace" is *charis*, which can also be translated as "kindness," "good will," "gift," or "thanks."[2] Theologian Ingrid Faro writes that "it has to do with favor, an expression or act of kindness without obligation."[3] Grace is one of the main themes of Jesus' parables and is foundational to the expression of God's character. When God describes Himself in Scripture, He says that He is "the compassionate and gracious God, slow to anger, abounding in love and faithfulness, maintaining love to thousands, and forgiving wickedness, rebellion and sin" (Exodus 34:6-7).

The grace-filled parables of Jesus were not just a teaching tool; they were integral to the life and ministry He incarnated. In his book *What's So Amazing about Grace?*, Philip Yancey writes that the parables were

the template of Jesus' life on earth. He was the shepherd who left the safety of the fold for the dark and dangerous night outside. To his banquets he welcomed tax collectors and reprobates and prostitutes. He came for the sick and not the well, for the unrighteous and not the righteous. And to those who betrayed him . . . he responded like a lovesick father.[4]

Often God's justice and truth are pitted against His mercy and grace, but truth and justice are inextricable aspects of God's character. As Faro puts it,

Mercy and grace become meaningless if they are unhinged from justice and righteousness. Justice is only as good as the moral character of the one who is judging. The first agency of action-consequence is rooted in the laws of nature and justice. But the greater agency of mercy and agency is at work, which intervenes and overrules the first when the appropriate conditions apply.

. . . [God] intervenes and redeems even the most-evil intentions of those who repent, and beautifully restores the lives of the faithful, even when they are marred by pain and the evil done against them. This pattern is portrayed throughout Scripture.[5]

God's redemptive plan culminates in the giving of His Son, Jesus Christ, who is the embodiment of God's grace and truth. The apostle John opens his Gospel with how "the Word became flesh and made his dwelling among us . . . full of grace and truth" (John 1:14)—and that "out of his fullness we have all received grace in place of grace already given" (John 1:16). In Jesus, there is no conflict between grace and truth. Jesus recognizes the consequences of sin in people's lives, but He doesn't condemn people for their sin. In accordance with God's just nature, Jesus fulfilled the requirements of the law by taking the condemnation of sin upon Himself on the cross, an act of pure, sacrificial love through which He extended us undeserved grace.

As the apostle Paul writes, "the grace of God has appeared that offers salvation to all people" (Titus 2:11). He points us to "Jesus Christ, who gave himself for us to redeem us from all wickedness and to purify for himself a people that are his very own, eager to do what is good" (Titus 2:13-14). God's grace and kindness draw us into a loving relationship with Him, which transforms us from the inside to live holy lives as His people—all by His grace.

My invitation to you is to read these parables slowly with fresh eyes and an open heart. If you allow the parables to sink deeply into your heart, they will expose the hidden facets of your values and challenge the way you see yourself, others, and the world. In addition, they will tear down walls you didn't realize existed, expanding your heart to embrace a more spacious, grace-filled Kingdom. My prayer is that these parables will be a gateway for you to encounter the God who loves you so much that He would leave the ninety-nine to find you, to tenderly heal your wounds and joyfully welcome you home! As a recipient of such grace and forgiveness, may you cultivate an ever-deepening loving relationship with God, one that causes you to overflow with grace toward others and demonstrate justice and mercy in the world.

THE SOWER

Grace to Those Who Have Ears to Hear (Luke 8:1-15)

FIRST-CENTURY PALESTINE was an agrarian society, which means that as soon as Jesus began to tell a parable about a farmer and seeds, His audience would have immediately pictured the situation: a farmer reaching his hand into a bag of seeds hanging from his neck or outer garment and scattering the seeds across the soil as he walked along his field. As he did this, seeds would fall on different kinds of soil. If the farmer was sowing to the edge of his field, some would inevitably fall along the adjacent path. So, too, would some fall on rocky soil, which was normal in the hills of Galilee. Everyone in first-century Palestine would have understood the importance of the farmer's work: The welfare of their society depended upon the outcome of the sowing.[1]

As He told this parable, Jesus was on His ministry tour, focused on "proclaiming the good news of the kingdom of God" (Luke 8:1). Following Jesus from town to town were the twelve apostles and a group of women who financially supported Jesus' ministry (Luke 8:2-3). Beyond that immediate circle, large crowds came to hear Jesus speak wherever He went. Some were looking to make Him a political king by force to free them from Roman oppression (John 6:14-15). Others sought Him because of the miracles and healings He performed. In town after town, crowds gathered around Him for various reasons. These diverse groups of people perhaps reflected the various types of soil represented in this parable about the sower.

But not everyone would understand the meaning of the parable, which Jesus then proceeded to explain to His disciples and those who had "ears to hear" (Luke 8:8). Jesus was teaching about the differing results of His preaching. Some people would reject Him outright. Others, while showing initial interest in following Him, were not prepared for the cost of discipleship in trials or suffering. The nature of the Kingdom Jesus preached is also not what people expected—it is "not about earthly power, conquest, and status, but rather the power of grace."[2]

But Jesus also saw the transformation of the disciples who heard the Word, believed, and persevered in their faith to bear fruit. The seed that fell on good soil yielded a crop, "a hundred times more than was sown" (Luke 8:8). As theologian Joachim Jeremias observes, "In spite of every failure and opposition, from hopeless beginnings, God brings forth the triumphant end which he had promised."[3]

"Sowing, though weak and vulnerable, is also something powerful and life-giving. As the seed brings a harvest of life-sustaining grain, though not overnight, so Jesus' word would produce the longed-for revolution of God."[4] The development of the different stages of the parable reflect how "Jesus' ministry was such a sowing: apparently ineffective, certainly vulnerable to rejection, yet still the initiation of the kingdom of God."[5]

1. Have you ever planted a seed and waited for it to bud or bear fruit? If so, what was that experience like? Why do you think Jesus applied the metaphor of sowing to His ministry?

2. There are four types of soil that the seeds fall upon in this story: the path, rocky ground, thorny soil, and good soil (Luke 8:5-8). Describe what happens to the seeds in each of the four scenarios.

____

____

____

____

____

____

____

____

According to New Testament scholar Darrell Bock, the parable of the sower should be called the "parable of the seed among the soils" or "responses to the word" because the major theme of the passage is the variety of responses to God's Word.[6] There is a decision to be faced when the Word is preached.[7]

3. Jesus said that in the parable the Word of God is the seed. How is the Kingdom of God initiated by sowing the Word? What can the seed of the Word produce?

____

____

____

____

____

____

____

____

____

The power of the Word that Jesus brought was "like seed, something creative, producing new life—the new life of the kingdom of God."[8] Isaiah 55:10-11 states, "As the rain and the snow / come down from heaven, / and do not return to it / without watering the earth / and making it bud and flourish, / so that it yields seed for the sower and bread for the eater, / so is my word that goes out from my mouth: / It will not return to me empty, / but will accomplish what I desire / and achieve the purpose for which I sent it."

"The kingdom is a kingdom of the word; it involves a proclamation about God and God's purposes and actions. Language creates a world, and the proclamation of the kingdom makes a new reality available. This is precisely what is happening with Jesus' preaching. The kingdom was being made a reality."[9]

The disciples have been given the secrets of the Kingdom of God. The Greek word translated "secrets" is *mystērion*, which in the New Testament refers to a secret revealed by God, as opposed to a natural human insight. Similarly, Ephesians 1:9 affirms that the mystērion of God's will involving Christ is now made known. "In order to really understand the gospel, we must be open to God's teaching, which may not be what we expect or can comprehend on our own."[10]

"Since the parables contain mysteries, they have a positive function for those who embrace Jesus. To those who do not embrace Jesus, the parables are not interpreted and thus remain enigmatic."[11] Luke 8:10 quotes Isaiah 6:9, a phrase that "alludes to judgment."[12] "God in judgment removes the benefit of revelation."[13] "The concealing takes place for those who are resistant to hearing" and "is a response to previous rejection of Jesus."[14]

4. Read Matthew 13:10-17. Why does Jesus say He speaks in parables? And what does he say the disciples have been given? (See Luke 8:9-10.)

____

____

____

____

____

____

____

____

5. As Jesus explained, the different kinds of soil represent hearers who receive the seed (the Word of God) in various ways. Consider the seed that falls on the path only to be trampled on or eaten by birds (Luke 8:5, 12). What are some things in your life situation right now that make it difficult for you to receive the Word of God? How can you "relocate" yourself to a place where you're not feeling as trampled on or as susceptible to negative influences that could lessen the impact of God's Word on your heart?

____

____

____

____

____

____

____

____

6. The seed that falls on the rocky soil grows but then withers during times of testing because the ground does not receive enough moisture (Luke 8:6, 13). Without judgment toward yourself or others who share from their personal experience, describe a time when you felt like your faith was being stretched. How did you respond?

First, someone who is good soil has an "honest and good heart," which contains "the idea of a moral quality and integrity." Second, good soil "hold[s] fast to the word, which is another way to speak of faith, since the verb portrays clinging to the word. One does not let go of commitment to God's promise; one perseveres in faith; one is unfailingly wedded to God's promise."[15] Third, good soil possesses patience, "a quality needed to bear up under the pressure of living faithfully. It is the opposite of falling away."[16]

Singer-songwriter Michael Card says that parables are "invitations to *shema*, to listen with everything you are. ('He who has ears, *shema*!' Jesus often says.)"[18] *Shema* is the Hebrew word for "hear" or "listen." The Shema is a Jewish prayer that is a central part of the morning and evening services. It is a prayer about listening to and loving God with everything you are: your heart, your soul, your strength.[19]

"A parable's ultimate aim is to awaken insight, stimulate the conscience, *and* move to action."[20]

7. Consider the seed that falls among thorns (Luke 8:7). This represents the situation where the hearers believe but the Word's impact and potential for flourishing are "choked by life's worries, riches and pleasures, and [the seeds] do not mature" (Luke 8:14). In what ways can you relate to this kind of seed?

____

____

____

____

____

____

____

____

____

8. The seed that falls on good soil yields a crop "a hundred times more than was sown" (Luke 8:8). In Jesus' context, the average yield of fields was 3.75-fold to 7.5-fold, and the average yield of individual seeds was 7.5- to 33-fold.[17] Read Luke 8:15 in a few different Bible translations. What are some qualities of the good soil?

____

____

____

____

____

____

____

____

9. A key theme in this parable is *hearing*—the idea is repeated seven times in this passage. However, hearing is not enough, since some people hear but do not understand (Luke 8:10). According to Jesus, you should "consider carefully *how* you listen" (Luke 8:18, emphasis added). Read the two stories that follow this parable in Luke 8:16-18 and Luke 8:19-21. What kind of listening is Jesus looking for? What should result from truly hearing and listening?

____

____

____

____

____

____

10. In this parable, the sower generously sows his seed on all kinds of soil. He does not restrict his sowing only to the areas that might produce the best harvest. How might this inform the way we do ministry or share the Word of God?

____

____

____

____

____

____

____

____

Author and podcast host Skye Jethani writes, "The indiscriminate sowing of seed in Jesus' story is a powerful vision of God's kingdom. He is saying that the kingdom is not a scarce commodity; it is not in limited supply nor does he restrict access to the kingdom to only those who will multiply it. Instead, the Lord casts the powerful seed of his kingdom far and wide, on the worthy and the unworthy, to both the righteous and the wicked. . . . The sower is focused on his immediate task of spreading the seed, rather than upon the outcome which is beyond his control."[21]

Your Response

It is possible to appear righteous, moral, and religious on the outside but be full of wickedness inside your heart (Mark 7:15-23). The Pharisees assumed that if the outside was clean, the inside would be clean as well. But Jesus chastised them for focusing on external behavior and failing to see that internal righteousness starts with the heart.[22] God extends His grace to all of us, but we can only receive it with a humble "noble and good" heart (Luke 8:15). Sometimes our own efforts and striving to be "righteous" can block us from receiving His grace.

Take a moment for reflection. What is the current condition of your heart? How is it affecting your relationship with God? Inhale slowly and pray, *Search my heart, O God,* then exhale slowly and pray, *Lead me in the way everlasting.* Repeat this breath prayer several times, allowing it to become a meditation that you can return to.

For Further Study

Sowing is a metaphor used often in Scripture. Read the parable of the seed growing secretly (Mark 4:26-29) and the parable of the mustard seed (Mark 4:30-32). Picture a plant that is growing and bearing fruit. Even though we can scientifically explain the process of how plants flourish, how this happens when it comes to our spiritual growth and flourishing is more mysterious. What role does grace play not only in our salvation but also in the process of our spiritual maturity and fruitfulness? What role does grace play in the growth of the Kingdom of God, yielding a harvest abundant beyond our imagination? How does the reality of grace keep us humble and dependent on God as we grow and mature?

THE LOST SHEEP AND THE LOST COIN

Grace to the Lost and Wandering (Luke 15:1-10)

IN JESUS' DAY, Jewish tax collectors were despised. Not only did they collect taxes for the Roman Empire—even to the point of utilizing Roman soldiers to enforce taxes—but they also earned a reputation for pocketing surcharges.[1] That's why it's striking that after Jesus says, "Whoever has ears to hear, let them hear" (Luke 14:35), the very next thing recorded by Luke is that those gathering around Jesus to *hear* Him are tax collectors and sinners (Luke 15:1). *Sinners* was a term used to refer to people of "low moral character."[2] The Pharisees and scribes looked down upon these two groups and were shocked that Jesus would welcome them.

The Pharisees were a large and influential Jewish religious party concerned with defining correct behavior according to the law. Their condemnation of Jesus' associations reflects the Old Testament warning not to associate with the godless (see Deuteronomy 21:20-21; Psalm 1:1). In their history, Israel failed to obey the law, fell into idolatry, and suffered the consequences of exile in Assyria and Babylon. The fervor of the Pharisees was due in part to their determination to prevent another disaster like this. However, "they made the law a burden for the people rather than something to teach and guide them." Theology professor Michelle Lee-Barnewall explains, "Instead of practicing justice and mercy (Mic 6:8), religious leaders came up with a legalistic interpretation that weighed the people down with duties and obligations."[3] Jesus accused them of being like "whitewashed tombs"—beautiful on the outside but spiritually dead on the inside (Matthew 23:27).

In Luke 15 the Pharisees and scribes are particularly appalled that Jesus would eat with the tax collectors and "sinners." During biblical times in the Middle East, table fellowship was a special sign of acceptance and honor[4]—"an offer of peace, trust, brotherhood and forgiveness; in short, sharing a table meant sharing life."[5] But sharing a meal with tax collectors and sinners also expresses an even deeper reality about Jesus' mission: It anticipates celebration of the banquet feast in Revelation, where sinners are included in the community of salvation.[6] This is "the most meaningful expression of the message of the redeeming love of God."[7]

When Jesus hears the Pharisees and scribes muttering about how He welcomes and eats with tax collectors and sinners, He tells three parables that reveal the Father's gracious heart for the lost: the lost sheep, the lost coin, and the lost sons. We will cover the first two in this session because they are both about seeking what has been lost, which shows how much Jesus values seeking sinners in the face of the Pharisees' and scribes' complaints.

1. Consider a time when you lost something valuable. What was your state of mind? Did you feel distressed? Anxious? Unable to focus on other things? If you found what you were looking for, how did your mood and mentality change?

____

____

____

____

____

____

____

____

2. The Pharisees thought they were pleasing God by how they followed the law. How did their focus on obeying the letter of the law rather than the heart underneath it blind them to their own need for grace? How did this in turn affect how they treated "sinners" and tax collectors?

____

____

____

____

____

____

____

____

____

In the ancient Middle East, women and shepherds were both considered low on society's social ladder. Women had few rights. Shepherds were poor and uneducated and would have been considered unclean by the Pharisees.[8] Middle Eastern and New Testament scholar Kenneth Bailey explains the significance of this: "If we accept that the parable was addressed to Pharisees (15:1-3), then the parable begins with a shock to their sensitivities. Any man who believed shepherds were unclean would naturally be offended if addressed as one."[9]

Yet the shepherd image is used in the Old Testament to describe Israelite leaders and to describe God's loving care for His people. Moreover, people who do not have a spiritual leader are referred to as sheep without a shepherd.[10]

3. Read the parables about the lost sheep (Luke 15:3-7) and the lost coin (Luke 15:8-10). Who are the unlikely heroes of these parables? What stands out to you about the status of these heroes?

____

____

____

____

____

____

____

4. Describe how the shepherd in the parable demonstrates his care for the one lost sheep (Luke 15:4-5).

____

____

____

____

____

____

"A lost sheep, we are told, usually lies down and gives up and will not find its way back. Possibly this is why the shepherd carries the sheep on his shoulders, but more likely it is intended to convey the care of a good shepherd. Images of shepherds carrying sheep are known from the various cultures long before Jesus."[11]

5. In what ways have you experienced God's pursuit of you? Have you ever felt like the sheep that the shepherd found and tenderly carried on his shoulders?

____

____

____

____

____

____

6. In the second parable we're studying in this session, what lengths does the woman go to in order to find her lost coin? How much is the coin worth (Luke 15:8)?

____

____

____

____

"The floors, which would have been either dirt or stone, would have been covered with straw as protection against cold and dampness. This meant that the woman would have had to remove the straw and sift through it, then sweep the floor."[12]

The coin "was equivalent to a denarius . . . a day's wage for an average worker." The coin could have been on a headdress that was part of a dowry.[13]

Joy and rejoicing are major themes of these parables. The shepherd and the woman call their respective communities to share in their joy through celebration, which matches the joy of heaven over a repentant sinner.

7. How do the shepherd and the woman both respond when they find what they are looking for (Luke 15:6, 9)? What does this tell you about the nature of joy?

____

____

____

____

____

____

____

____

The Pharisees and scribes needed to repent of their self-righteousness, but their failure to recognize their need for repentance made them unreachable. "The Pharisees should have remembered Isaiah's words, 'All we like sheep have gone astray' (Isaiah 53:6)."[14]

"Those who recognize where they stand before God and respond accordingly are the cause of great joy in heaven."[15]

8. Both parables end with God and the heavenly hosts rejoicing over each sinner who repents. Repentance is equated with being found and is a great cause of joy! Reflect on a time when you wandered away from God, either before you came to Christ or when you were caught in a pattern of sin even after knowing Him. What did you experience when you repented? How have you felt God's joy when you've allowed Him to find you?

____

____

____

____

____

____

____

9. What do these parables reveal about God's character?

____

____

____

____

____

____

____

____

____

____

"What is revealed about the character of God is the value he places on even the least deserving and the care he extends to such people. God is not passive, waiting for people to approach him after they get their lives in order. . . . Unquestionably, God will seek the lost and restore them. Seeking and joy are the twin pillars of the parable [of the lost sheep], and God's seeking does not come with conditions attached. The joy reflects both the attitude of God at recovering the lost and the celebration of the kingdom with its good news that God's promised redemption has begun."[16]

10. Jesus was inviting the Pharisees to rejoice with Him over the tax collectors and sinners coming to Him. What is your posture toward others who may seem undeserving of God's grace? What can make it difficult to rejoice in the grace others receive? What might your reaction reveal about your own heart?

____

____

____

____

____

____

____

____

____

"What is infectiously appealing about Jesus is that he likes to celebrate. He is consistently meeting people not at the altar but at table, whether as host, guest, or the body and blood to be consumed. . . . He is indiscriminate in his dining companions, who include Pharisees, tax collectors, sinners, and even an upscale family consisting of two sisters and a formerly dead brother. . . . To be in his presence is not only to be challenged and comforted; it is to celebrate at table."[17]

11. What we choose to celebrate often reflects our values or what the culture around us celebrates. What do you want to celebrate more in your life or family? Share some ideas of how you can intentionally celebrate those things.

____

____

____

____

____

____

____

Your Response

How would you define *grace* in your own words? How was your understanding of this concept influenced by your family of origin and the way you were parented? If you have a religious background, what kind of theology were you taught around grace? Has your understanding of grace evolved? If so, how? What is the current posture of your heart toward God's grace to you? Use your answers to these questions to journal a short paragraph about your understanding of grace. Then ask God to help you receive His lavish grace for you.

____

____

____

____

____

____

____

____

____

____

____

For Further Study

Read about the restoration of Israel's remnant in
Zephaniah 3:9-20. The prophet Zephaniah preached
the need to seek the Lord in light of the approaching
judgment of Judah due to their wicked and idolatrous
practices. Yet in these verses he also delivers a message of hope that God will establish a remnant of
His people. What are some similarities between the
Luke 15 parables we've studied in this session and
this passage in Zephaniah? Pay special attention to
Zephaniah 3:17-20.

____

____

____

____

____

____

____

____

____

____

____

THE PRODIGAL FATHER

Grace to the Lost Sons (Luke 15:11-32)

THE TITLE OF A PARABLE influences what we hear and what lessons we glean. This story is most often known as "the parable of the prodigal son," but that title causes us to focus primarily on the main character of the first half of the story: the younger son, who takes his share of the inheritance, leaves home, and leads a reckless and wasteful life. We should not miss, however, that the rest of the narrative is about the father and the older son.

Jesus did not downplay the younger son's sin. We must understand the ramifications of what the younger son does to appreciate how incredible the father's response is. Culturally, an Israelite father would be expected to discipline or even reject a son who has lost the family inheritance among the Gentiles.[1] The community would publicly shame him as well,[2] subjecting him to a ceremony called *kezazah*, which literally means "the cutting off." They would break a large pot in front of him and proclaim that he was cut off from his people. He would have no rights to claim, and no one would take him in.[3] When the younger son in this story loses his inheritance in a faraway Gentile land, he knows that he has burned all his bridges—not only with his family but also with his entire village. Insomuch as the younger son represents sinners, "he portrays their position as one of outrageous, selfish rebellion against a loving father, the result of which is that they are in a 'far country', 'lost' and (strikingly) 'dead.'"[4]

But the older son, too, is in rebellion against his father. Even though the older son never leaves home, he is emotionally distant from the father. The older son uses no title of respect when he addresses the father, accuses him of favoritism, and sees himself as a slave rather than a son.[5] Ingrid Faro writes,

> Outwardly he was doing all the right things, but inwardly he was resentful and bitter toward his father and his brother and lacked love and mercy. . . . [He] stayed behind [and] did what was expected, but his heart was cold.
> . . . We are only capable of freely giving to others what we have first freely received ourselves. . . . Those who are judgmental and unable to give mercy and grace may have never freely received the goodness of God.[6]

Thus, both sons venture away from a loving relationship with their father—the younger son by fleeing in rebellion before returning home; the older son through his bitterness, resentment, and self-righteousness, which prevent him also from experiencing the goodness of his father.

While *prodigal* can be defined as "wayward" or "foolish," it can also mean "recklessly extravagant." Certainly the father in this parable is prodigal in terms of the lavish grace he pours out upon both undeserving sons. Perhaps a better title for this parable would be "the parable of the prodigal father and his two lost sons." As you study this parable, consider how both sons are lost and how the father's love and grace toward each is reckless, extravagant, and astonishing!

1. The younger son has to reach rock bottom before he comes home to the father. Describe a time when you or someone you know returned to God. What did it take for you or them to come home?

____

____

____

____

____

____

____

____

____

The younger son's inheritance would be a third of the total inheritance, which he would not normally receive until his father's death. Even if the father gave the property over to his sons while he was still alive, the cultural understanding was that the father would continue to have use of it until he died. By demanding his share and leaving with it, the younger son is ignoring his responsibility to care for his father and treating him as though he is already dead.[7] In doing so, the younger son is breaking fellowship with his father, the family clan, and the entire village. "A man with no such roots is considered a vagabond and is not trusted."[8]

2. Read the parable of the lost sons (Luke 15:11-32). What do you think the younger son's request for his share of the estate communicates to the father (Luke 15:12)?

____

____

____

____

____

____

____

____

3. Describe what happens to the younger son after he goes to a distant land and "squander[s] his wealth in wild living" (Luke 15:13; also see verses 14-16). Do you think the son is truly repentant? Why or why not?

____

____

____

____

____

____

____

____

"The 'distant country' was apparently outside strictly Jewish territory, and the wayward son found himself with the demeaning job of feeding pigs (v. 15)—unclean animals for the Jews."[9] He even desires to eat the food that the pigs are fed, which shows how far he has fallen. Bailey writes, "He has no genuine humility; he just wants to eat."[10]

4. What does the younger son plan to say to his father upon returning home? What does his speech reveal about his understanding of their relationship?

____

____

____

____

____

____

____

____

The younger son has a face-saving plan "that will give him independence from his father and provide an opportunity to compensate for his errors. With pride intact he intends to order his father to make him a hired servant."[11] Author Ann Voskamp writes, "How often am I the prodigal trying to find a way to work and earn my way back, work for Abba instead of be with Abba, perform impressively enough for Abba, instead of passionately living with Abba, in Abba? . . . You can look like you're going God's way while your heart is still going its own way. You can want God's ways—but you can want your own ways more."[12]

The father's dramatic actions shield the son from the animosity of the village and repair his reputation among them.[13] Perhaps the father is watching for his son and runs (which was regarded as undignified for older men to do in ancient Palestinian culture) to get there before the other villagers. Thus the father shames himself so that the son will not be shamed. In this act of love we see the Cross of Jesus Christ, who shamed Himself so that we would not be shamed.[14]

The father gives the younger son the "best robe" (Luke 15:22), which is perhaps the father's own that he wears on special occasions. The father gives him a ring, perhaps a signet ring, signifying that he is trusted with authority. The father places shoes on his feet, distinguishing him from slaves (who would not wear shoes).[15] Further, the fattened calf would be enough to feed over a hundred people and would normally have been reserved for a grand occasion, like a wedding.[16]

5. What strikes you about how the father greets the younger son (Luke 15:20)? What does this reaction reveal about the father's heart?

____

____

____

____

____

____

6. What is significant about the gifts the father lavishes upon the younger son (Luke 15:22-24)?

____

____

____

____

____

7. Put yourself in the shoes of the younger brother. What would it be like to receive the father's embrace and these gifts?

____

____

____

____

____

8. Compare the speech the son has prepared (Luke 15:18-19) with what he actually says to the father (Luke 15:21). What may be stopping the son from including everything he planned to say?

Either the father interrupts the son midspeech or the son realizes that he doesn't need to finish what he planned to say in the face of his loving father.

____

____

____

____

____

____

____

____

____

____

9. How does the older son respond when he discovers that his father is throwing a party to celebrate his brother's homecoming (Luke 15:28-30)? How does he view his relationship with his father?

____

____

____

____

____

____

____

____

____

In contrast to the older son, who does not address him with a title, the father calls him "my son" (Luke 15:31). "After assuring his elder son of their perpetual bond, the father then attempts to restore, or create, a relationship between the two children. Correcting the elder's phrase 'your son, this one' to 'your brother, this one,' the father reminds his child that the relationship exists between the two of them. Were either brother to be missing, the family would not be whole."[18]

"This parable is not merely about relations with God but . . . sets the pattern for dealing with human relations and estrangement as well. We cannot claim to be returning to the Father without displaying the same kind of forgiveness and willingness to embrace which the Father displays."[19]

10. The older son refuses to come into the party (Luke 15:28), which would be considered a public insult against the father.[17] Instead of scolding the older son for his disrespectful behavior, how does the father talk to him (Luke 15:31-32)? What does this reveal about the father's heart toward both his sons?

____

____

____

____

____

____

____

____

11. The older son's response is not recorded in the parable, perhaps to allow the Pharisees to picture themselves in his shoes. If you were among the Pharisees who heard the three parables in Luke 15, how might you respond?

____

____

____

____

____

____

____

____

Your Response

Both sons fail to understand the father's love and grace
for them, instead thinking that they have to work to
earn their place in the family. In his prepared speech,
the younger son plans to ask the father to make him
"like one of [his] hired servants" (Luke 15:19). The older
son also thinks of himself as a slave, working all these
years for the father (Luke 15:29). How we view God
and our relationship with Him determines how we
respond to Him. Describe your view of God and how
you've come to view Him this way. Is He like a harsh
boss, a distant figure, a loving father, or something
else to you? Now spend some time in silence. Ask God
to reveal five words that describe how He wants to
relate to you. Then ask Him to reveal five words of
affirmation that describe how He sees you.

For Further Study

Read Ephesians 2:1-10. What themes in the parable of the lost sons are echoed in Paul's letter to the Christians in Ephesus? What similarities do you see between the father in the parable and God in this passage?

THE GOOD SAMARITAN

Grace to the Neighbor and the Wounded (Luke 10:25-37)

A FEW VERSES BEFORE the parable of the Good Samaritan, Luke records Jesus' words that God has hidden things from the "wise and learned, and revealed them to little children" (Luke 10:21). It doesn't seem coincidental that the parable is an answer to a learned man, an expert in the law asking Jesus what he must do to inherit eternal life. This question was meant to test Jesus (Luke 10:25), perhaps to see if He would give an answer aligned with the law. Theologian Klyne R. Snodgrass notes that "Jesus' association with outcasts and sinners, his actions on the Sabbath, and his lack of concern for such 'holiness' issues as touching the unclean" probably raised questions for this lawyer as to where Jesus stood in relation to the law.[1]

As Jesus often did, He responded to the question with another question: "What is written in the Law? . . . How do you read it?" (Luke 10:26). The expert in the law answered by reciting Deuteronomy 6:5 ("Love the LORD your God with all your heart and with all your soul and with all your strength") and Leviticus 19:18 ("Love your neighbor as yourself").

When Jesus responded that the lawyer had answered correctly and should follow this teaching, the lawyer came back with another question: "Who is my neighbor?" (Luke 10:29). First-century Judaism ordered relationships and responsibilities according to a series of concentric circles. Michelle Lee-Barnewall explains,

If the Jew were at the center, the expanding circles would include first immediate relatives, then kinsmen, and then all other Jews. Foundational to the circles was determining who was worthy of aid based on self-interest and ethnic belonging. Lines were drawn so that those inside received help while those outside did not.[2]

Moreover, at that time, Judaism stressed religious and social separation from "unclean" people, including "sinners," tax collectors, lepers, Gentiles, and Samaritans.[3] Jesus' treatment of these "unclean" people was blurring these boundaries. The parable that Jesus proceeded to tell demonstrates that while the lawyer's answer was technically correct, his reading of the law did not help him understand the heart of God.

Jews despised the Samaritans and considered them racially and ritually unclean. The Samaritans had originated from intermarriage between Jews and Assyrians following Assyria's conquest of the northern kingdom of Israel in about 721 BC.[4] The Samaritans were also seen as having a compromised faith. They had their own unique version of the first five books of Scripture and rejected the Prophets and some of the other writings of the Hebrew Bible.[5]

1. When you hear the phrase *Good Samaritan*, what do you think of? This phrase would have been considered an oxymoron by the Jews living in Jesus' time. Why do you think that is?

____

____

____

____

____

____

____

____

____

____

2. The parable was told after the expert of the law asked Jesus what he must do to inherit eternal life. He already knew what the law says about loving the Lord and loving your neighbor. Why do you think he asked Jesus, "Who is my neighbor?"

____

____

____

____

____

____

____

"The only way this man (or any person) can 'justify himself' is to limit the extent of the Law's demand and consequently limit his own responsibility."[6]

"Any disagreement between Jesus and his contemporaries was not over the significance of the love commands but over their application and extent. How far does love of neighbor reach? This parable is evidence of what is obvious elsewhere: Jesus will not allow boundaries to be set so that people may feel they have completed their obligation to God. Love does not have a boundary where we can say we have loved enough, nor does it permit us to choose those we will love, those who are 'our kind.'"[7]

Jesus' audience would have been familiar with the dangerous conditions of the road from Jerusalem to Jericho. It descended sharply and curved through rocky terrain where bandits could hide.[8] Jesus told His listeners that the man traveling along this road was wounded by a seemingly random act of violence. But He did not provide details about the victim's ethnicity, class, religion, or anything else that listeners could use to determine whether he was "deserving" of help.

3. Why do you think Jesus only identified the man by what happened to him?

____

____

____

____

____

____

Perhaps Jesus left demographic details out because the "neighbor" we are supposed to help is anyone who is in need.

The priests were in charge of the sacrifices of the Temple, and the Levites were second-ranking figures who assisted them in Temple services and order. Touching a dead person would make the priest ceremonially unclean, preventing him from performing his Temple duties (see Leviticus 21:1, 11). The priest in this parable may not want to risk becoming defiled, even though it is unclear to him whether the man is still alive. Rules for Levites were more lenient, but this one may also be wishing to avoid becoming unclean.[9] But it is interesting to note that they are headed away from Jerusalem (Luke 10:30) and thus have finished the Temple duties that would require ritual cleanliness.[10]

"The first question that the [priest and] Levite asked was, 'If I stop to help this man, what will happen to me?' But then the Good Samaritan came by. And he reversed the question: 'If I do not stop to help this man, what will happen to him?'"[11]

Allowing ourselves to see other people in their humanity and to feel compassion for them is a precursor for action. The same word for "have compassion" (*splanchnizomai*) is used in the parable of the prodigal son, where the father, seeing his son a long way off, "was filled with compassion for him" (Luke 15:20). It is also the same word that describes how Jesus had compassion for the crowds when He saw them "because they were harassed and helpless, like sheep without a shepherd" (Matthew 9:36).

"The parable underscores that compassion (the turning point of the parable, v. 33), mercy, and love are the key factors in living for God (and therefore in discipleship to Jesus)."[12]

4. Who sees the wounded man but passes by on the other side of the road? What excuses might they have for not stopping to help the man?

____

____

____

____

____

____

____

____

5. In contrast, what does the Samaritan do when he first comes upon the wounded man (Luke 10:33)?

____

____

____

____

____

____

____

____

____

____

6. What does the Samaritan do to help (Luke 10:34-35)? What is he risking by helping the wounded man?

Two denarii was equal to two day's wages.[13] This is very generous considering it is possible that two denarii would have covered about two weeks of room and board.[14]

7. Why do you think Jesus made the Samaritan the hero of the story?

Jesus challenged the long-standing enmity between Jews and Samaritans and demolished all boundaries of social position, such as race, religion, and region.[15]

The parable exposed the lawyer's own self-righteousness and his prejudice toward the Samaritan. He could not even bring himself to say "the Samaritan" but only said "the one who had mercy on him" (Luke 10:37). "Jesus has turned the issue from the boundaries of required neighborliness to the essential nature of neighborliness."[16] Moreover, love "does not allow limits on the definition of neighbor"[17] and is demonstrated through concrete actions of mercy and love.

"The question of identity is never merely a question of what we believe as fact, but what we *are*, particularly what we are in relation to God and what motivates us and controls our being. We have torn thinking from being and being from doing, but what we are cannot be torn from what we do. . . . The idea of knowing God and yet not being conformed to God is a source of scandal, one that Scripture always combats and that modern Christians must combat as well. In the parable Jesus seeks to make a man of knowledge into a man of practice, for anything less is not sufficient for eternal life. This is not a question of earning salvation; it is a question of being and identity that determine actions."[18]

8. At the end of the parable, Jesus did not focus on the object of neighborly love (the victim), but rather turned the lawyer's question upside down by asking him which of these three was a neighbor to the man who fell into the hands of robbers. How did the lawyer answer Jesus' question (Luke 10:37)? What does his reply reveal about his prejudice?

____

____

____

____

____

____

____

9. The lawyer's initial question was about what he must *do* to inherit eternal life. In Luke 10:28, Jesus tells the lawyer, "Do this and you will live," and similarly in Luke 10:37, Jesus says, "Go and do likewise." Summarize what Jesus was telling the lawyer he must do. How would this shatter the lawyer's perceived religious system?

____

____

____

____

____

____

____

10. Think of someone people could easily pass by without really seeing. Perhaps they are wounded and needy, or perhaps they are someone we might even consider an enemy. This could be a person or group of people. Pray and ask God to give you eyes to see the "Samaritans" in your life and be moved with compassion. What are some steps you can take to build a relationship with such a person or group of people?

Your Response

Read the parable again, this time putting yourself in the shoes of the wounded man left half dead on the side of the road. What emotions do you feel as the story unfolds? Imagine that you are conscious and aware but not strong enough to cry out for help. What goes through your mind as the priest and Levite pass you by? How do you feel as you receive the Samaritan's care and kindness? How does the Samaritan's extravagant care reflect God's care and grace? Now picture God tenderly pouring out His healing oil (or love) on your wounds. Say a prayer thanking God for His grace to you.

For Further Study

The Jews and the Samaritans strongly disagreed about the proper place of worship, whether at the Temple in Jerusalem or atop Mount Gerizim in Samaria.[19] But Jesus announced to the Samaritan woman at the well that "a time is coming and has now come when the true worshipers [Jews and Samaritans alike] will worship the Father in the Spirit and in truth" (John 4:23). Then, for the first time in the Gospels, Jesus reveals His identity as the long-awaited Messiah (John 4:26). Jesus knocks down barriers that separate people from Him and does away with divisions among people. What is the significance of Jesus choosing a Samaritan woman to be the first to hear the good news that He is the Messiah? What does this reveal about His Kingdom?

THE TWO DEBTORS

Grace to the Forgiven
(Luke 7:36-50)

SIMON THE PHARISEE INVITED JESUS to his house for a special meal. In first-century Palestine, people often hosted meals for religious study. Jesus was known in the community, so the Pharisee likely invited Him as a "visiting sage" to engage Him in theological discussion.[1]

Even though Simon had asked Jesus to come to his home, he neglected to extend the common customs of hospitality to Jesus. In the Middle East during that time, formal greetings carried great significance. The host would greet an honored guest or a rabbi with a kiss. Anointing with oil was also common, though its omission would probably have been less offensive.[2] The host or his servant would wash the guest's feet,[3] or at the very least provide water for the guest to wash his own feet. Simon's failure to do any of these things for Jesus was unmistakably insulting.[4]

During the dinner, an unexpected visitor arrived. A woman who led a "sinful life" had found out that Jesus was at the Pharisee's house, and she entered the banquet (Luke 7:37). New Testament scholar Darrell Bock explains that "at special meals the door was left open, so uninvited guests could enter, sit by the walls, and hear the conversation."[5] Some commentators believe that this woman was a prostitute because she is referred to as "a woman of the city" (Luke 7:37, ESV), but she may instead have been "the wife of someone with a dishonorable occupation, a woman in debt, or an adulteress."[6]

The passage states that Jesus reclined at the table, which was "the normal position for eating" at a banquet. A person would "lie on his side, facing the table, and with body and feet angling away from the table."[7] The woman approached Jesus, humbly positioned herself at His feet, and then proceeded to give Him the kind of tribute ordinarily reserved for noblemen or royalty.[8] Simon condemned Jesus for allowing this woman to make such a scene over Him. Jesus then proceeded to tell him a parable about two debtors.

---

1. Describe a time when you were forgiven for something. How did that impact your relationship with the person who forgave you?

____

____

____

____

____

____

2. This woman who lived a "sinful life" entered the banquet of men and lavished Jesus with an offering of love (Luke 7:37-38). What did the woman do? What do you think compelled her to act?

____

____

____

____

____

____

According to theologian Kenneth Bailey, "she is offering her love *and* trying to compensate for the insult that Jesus has just received."[9] After witnessing how Simon did not even give Jesus a proper greeting or water to wash His feet, she was overcome. When she could not greet Jesus with a kiss, she kissed His feet. Then she spontaneously washed His feet with her tears. Having no towel, she let down her hair to wipe His feet. It would be too presumptuous for a sinful woman to anoint the head of a rabbi, so she brought a flask of perfume to pour on Jesus' feet.[10]

"Touching or caressing a man's feet could have sexual overtones, as did letting down her hair, so a woman never let down her hair in public. Moreover, the woman was known to be a sinner. Assuming she was unclean, she would have made Jesus unclean by touching him."[11] However, "women sometimes let their hair down for other reasons, especially to show religious devotion/ gratitude or grief, either of which could be operative here."[12]

3. How could her actions have been misunderstood and even considered scandalous?

____

____

____

____

____

____

____

____

____

4. Simon viewed this woman as impure and her actions as defiling Jesus (Luke 7:39). The Pharisee could not see beyond the woman's past to appreciate her heart of repentance and acceptance of grace. What do you think contributed to Simon's blindness toward the woman? What would be at stake if he were to shed his blindness and see the woman as Jesus did?

____

____

____

____

____

____

____

____

5. Simon doubted that Jesus was a prophet based on how He received the woman (Luke 7:39). In what ways does Jesus show that He is a prophet—and even more than a prophet—in this passage?

____

____

____

____

____

____

____

____

By knowing both Simon's thoughts and the character of the woman, Jesus demonstrates that He is a prophet. By announcing the forgiveness of her sins in Luke 7:48, He shows that He is greater than a prophet.[13]

In Luke 5, before Jesus healed the man with paralysis, He told him that his sins were forgiven. The religious leaders' response was similar in that situation: "Who is this fellow who speaks blasphemy? Who can forgive sins but God alone?" (Luke 5:21).

6. The parable that Jesus tells Simon in Luke 7:41-42 is short and straightforward. A man forgives the debts of two people who owe him vastly different amounts. Which of the two debtors loves him more, and why?

____

____

____

____

____

____

____

____

____

____

"The *denarius*, a Roman silver coin, was the typical day's wage."[14] If the average salary today is about $59,000 per year,[15] then the debt would be about $80,821 (500 denarii) versus $8,082 (50 denarii).

"The verb used for forgiving the debt, χαρίζομαι (*charizomai*), was a common business term for remitting debt and is the very verb that will picture later in Scripture the free offer of God's grace. . . . It is the unmerited character of the act that is the basis for the gratitude."[16]

"It is formed from the word *charis* ('grace'), [which] often means 'give graciously,' and is used in the Pauline letters for forgiveness of sins."[17]

"God is ready and willing to forgive the debts of people and to act graciously beyond expectation. This picture of God's grace motivates Jesus' acceptance of those in dire need and his openness toward sinners. It is this very point that Simon needs to see."[18]

7. What was Jesus' intent in comparing the amount of sin forgiven and the amount of love expressed? Did He mean that we should sin more so we can love Him more? Why or why not?

____

____

____

____

____

____

____

____

____

____

8. By contrasting the woman's love and devotion with Simon's lack of hospitality, Jesus was commending a "sinful" woman and criticizing a "respectable" man of the community in front of all the other guests (Luke 7:44-46). How might Jesus' words have challenged the prevailing cultural and gender views of the time?

____

____

____

____

____

____

____

9. After Simon answered correctly, Jesus asked if he saw "this woman" (Luke 7:44). Simon stereotyped her and saw only her reputation, not the woman herself. Describe a time when God helped you see someone in a new light. What changed your preconceived notion or first impression of the person?

____

____

____

____

____

____

____

____

____

____

The story of Hagar in Genesis reminds us that God sees each of us, no matter what we have been through. "God is present in the center of our trauma . . . and he will not leave any of his children's stories without a redemptive ending."[22] Hagar was a female slave and a foreigner who was forced to sleep with Abram to conceive a child for Abram and Sarai (Genesis 16:1-4). She was abused by Sarai and fled to the desert, where God met her (Genesis 16:6-7). "She was also the only person in the entire Bible who was given a voice and a platform to name God,"[23] saying, "You are the God who sees me. . . . I have now seen the One who sees me" (Genesis 16:13).

10. Before you can receive forgiveness, you must first realize that you are in need of forgiveness. The woman's act of love showed her realization of her forgiven status. Simon's inability to see that he needed to be forgiven much blocked him from receiving the grace the woman received. What did Simon need forgiveness for?

____

____

____

____

____

____

"Simon focuses on the external part of the law and sees himself as righteous. He does not realize that in terms of sins of the heart, he is in great need of forgiveness."[24]

Those sins of the heart could include "pride, arrogance, hard-heartedness, hostility, a judgmental spirit, slim understanding of what really defiles, a rejection of sinners, insensitivity, misunderstanding of the nature of God's forgiveness, and sexism."[25]

"In this passage love is understood as the expression of faith (cf. Gal 5:6), and properly understood it is difficult to imagine faith that does not involve love. To love God with the whole heart, mind, and strength is not something less than faith, and faith cannot accomplish more. Faith will love, or it is not faith."[26]

11. In this passage, the woman's actions demonstrate the relationship between faith and love. How would you describe the connection between faith and love?

Your Response

Our capacity to love God is related to our ability to receive His grace, forgiveness, and love. Often we, like Simon, can focus on external sins. Ask God to reveal if there are any sins of the heart preventing you from accepting His grace and forgiveness. Repent of anything that you need to confess, knowing that God welcomes and forgives you. Now imagine you hear the same words from Jesus that He spoke to the woman: "Your sins are forgiven" and "Your faith has saved you; go in peace" (Luke 7:48, 50).

For Further Study

Read the parable of the unforgiving servant in Matthew 18:21-35. Like the woman in this parable, he is also forgiven much. What is his response? What does his treatment of others reveal about his ability to receive and give love and grace? Even though he is forgiven of a great debt, how is he more like Simon the Pharisee than the woman who received grace?

THE PERSISTENT WIDOW

Grace to Those Who Persevere (Luke 18:1-8)

IN FIRST-CENTURY PALESTINE, widows were on the lowest rung of society, along with orphans and foreigners. They often did not have the means to support themselves.[1] If a widow's husband had owned property, she might be provided for, but the property would not be passed down to her. If she stayed in her husband's family, she would be treated as second-class. Some widows were even sold into slavery.[2]

Jesus regularly upended cultural expectations and biases in His parables, and this parable is no exception: Not only does He elevate a woman as a model for His disciples to follow, but that woman is a widow who demonstrates self-advocacy and persistence. This widow pleads her own case before a judge in a cultural context where normally only men spoke in the courtroom and women needed a male advocate to plead cases for them.[3] This woman lacks money, power, and a male advocate to speak on her behalf. Middle Eastern and New Testament scholar Kenneth Bailey describes the court as a place where men shouted and pushed to get the judge's attention,[4] so perhaps this widow even has to shout loudly to be heard over the men. Moreover, she also probably knows that the judge has a reputation for being harsh and uncompassionate. Her adversary likely has more influence over the judge than she does. Yet despite these circumstances, she persists and does not give up.

The widow's specific request isn't stated, but most likely it has to do with "a debt, a pledge, or a portion of an inheritance [that] is being withheld from her."[5] The parable assumes that the widow is being denied what is right and that for some reason the judge does not initially want to listen to her.

The unjust judge in this parable stands in contrast to God, who is just and compassionate. New Testament scholar Craig Keener writes,

> This parable is a standard Jewish "how much more" (*qal vahomer*) argument: if an unjust judge who cared not for widows can dispense justice, how much more will the righteous judge of all the earth, who was known as the defender of widows and orphans, do so? . . . The principle is familiar from the Old Testament: God is faithful to act on behalf of and to vindicate his people, by his acts in the present and especially his final day of judgment.[6]

God is not reluctant to hear the cries of His people. He is full of grace and will bring justice to those who call out to Him.

Jesus told this parable to His disciples knowing that they would face increasing adversity as He journeyed toward the Cross. After His death, the disciples would need to persevere in their faith through severe persecution to establish the early church. He wanted them to know that God would graciously answer them when they cried out to Him in prayer and did not give up. The parable of the persistent widow would help prepare them for what lay ahead.

---

1. Have you prayed for something over and over again? What tempts you to give up? What helps you persevere in prayer?

____

____

____

____

____

____

____

2. What is the reputation of this judge (Luke 18:2)? How does he describe himself (verse 4)?

____

____

____

____

____

____

____

____

____

____

____

"The judge is probably a Jew and may have been a powerful man, since the Romans allowed the Jews to manage many of their own legal affairs," except those involving capital punishment.[7]

The word *entrepō* in Luke 18:2, which many translations render "to respect," can also mean "to make ashamed." The Middle East has an honor-shame culture. The problem with the judge is not that he fails to respect other people but that he feels no shame. He should feel ashamed that he is hurting a destitute widow, but there is no spark of honor left in his soul to which others can appeal.[8]

3. Read Proverbs 1:7. What does it mean to fear God? Why would this be important for a judge in ancient Israel?

____

____

____

____

____

____

____

____

____

____

"In ancient Israel, the duty of a judge was to maintain harmonious relations and adjudicate disputes between Israelites."[9] "The judge's responsibility within the covenant community, therefore, was to declare God's judgment and establish *shalom* among God's people. Jehoshaphat's charge to the judges of his day included a warning to 'let the fear of the LORD be upon you' (2 Chr 19:7)."[10]

4. Read Exodus 34:5-7, where God describes His character. What do you notice about what God is like from these verses? Given the difference between God and the unjust judge, contrast the judge's attitude toward the widow with what you believe God's posture and attitude is toward you when you approach Him.

____

____

____

____

____

____

____

____

____

"God . . . is *not* like the uncaring, unrighteous judge, but is merciful, patient, and eager to assist his people."[11] Therefore, we can pray and not lose heart because we know what God is like, that He is "working in a comprehensive kingdom way, and we want to be in on the work."[12]

Commentaries disagree on the interpretation of the question in Luke 18:7: "Will he delay long over them?" (ESV).[13] But however long the delay is, there is assurance in verse 8 that God does hear the cries of His people and that He will speedily (*en tachei*) bring vindication for them. *En tachei* could mean "suddenly" or "soon," perhaps referring to Jesus' return.[14]

5. Luke 18:7-8 describes how God responds to those who cry out to Him day and night. How does that give you hope and help you pray?

____

____

____

____

____

____

____

____

6. How is the widow described in Luke 18:3? What does she seek?

____

____

____

____

____

____

____

____

____

____

Most translations state that the widow is seeking justice, but in this context, the Greek term in Luke 18:3 (*ekdikeō*) might be better understood as "avenged." According to scholar Amy-Jill Levine, "the language is juridical . . . it has the connotation of 'to set things right' or 'to be vindicated.'"[15]

Vindication has begun with the Kingdom and the Resurrection but awaits Jesus' return and final judgment and ultimate vindication. There is a tension between *now* and *not yet*.[16]

7. Read Romans 12:17-21. Paul commands his readers not to take revenge but to "leave room for God's wrath" (verse 19). Have you experienced the desire to seek vengeance? What did you choose to do? What can we learn from the widow's example?

____

____

____

____

____

____

____

____

The widow is not gentle and docile; she wears down the judge by her relentless requests. In Luke 18:5, "the Greek uses a boxing term: the judge is concerned that the widow will give him a black eye."[17] According to Kenneth Bailey, the woman was probably not literally violent, because in that culture, she would be forcibly removed from the courtroom and not allowed back. But according to the rich Arabic translation tradition, she was irritating him so much that it was like a blow to the head, giving him a headache.[18]

Prayer can be agonizingly urgent, intense, and earnest. We are to pray with "faith, patience, and persistence."[19]

Pastor and theologian Eugene Peterson also notes the difference Evagrius points out between "persevering in 'our prayer'" and "persisting in 'my petition,'" which can be a lack of surrender to God's will and a license to be disobedient.[20] Knowing that God's nature is good helps us surrender to His will.

8. Why does the judge give in to the widow's pleas (Luke 18:5)?

____

____

____

____

____

____

____

____

____

9. Sometimes we think our prayers to God should be polite. Or perhaps we stop presenting our requests to God because He already knows what we want. What can we learn about prayer from the way the widow petitions the judge?

____

____

____

____

____

____

____

____

____

10. How does God's compassionate and just nature influence how we relate to Him in prayer?

____

____

____

____

____

____

____

____

____

11. The parable ends with the question of whether Jesus will find faith on earth when He returns (Luke 18:8). What do you think the point of this question is in relation to the parable?

____

____

____

____

____

____

____

____

____

The Greek reads "will he find *the* faith on the earth?" (Luke 18:8). The first instance of the definite article, *the*, appears to suggest that "Christ is referring to the specific kind of faith just illustrated [by the widow]."[21] When the Son of Man returns, He will be looking for those who are looking for Him. Jesus is calling for a faith that keeps praying, seeking justice, and tenaciously following Him.[22]

Your Response

Read David's prayer in Psalm 31 asking God to deliver him from his enemies. David does not hold back from expressing how desperate he feels and how much he longs for God's deliverance. He approaches God knowing that God is righteous, faithful, merciful, and just. David concludes his prayer by saying, "Be strong and take heart, / all you who hope in the LORD" (verse 24). Write your own prayer honestly expressing your feelings to God. Cry out to Him for help because you can approach His throne of grace with confidence (Hebrews 4:16)!

For Further Study

Read Luke 11:5-13. How is the parable of the friend at midnight similar to the parable of the persistent widow? What do you make of the phrase "shameless audacity" in verse 8, which is used in a positive sense in this passage? Where in your life do you need to approach God with more shameless audacity? What would it look like for you to do that?

THE LABORERS IN THE VINEYARD

Grace to the Undeserving
(Matthew 20:1-16)

THE KINGDOM OF HEAVEN is the realm where God rules. God is intervening in history not only to bring salvation but also to establish His reign over everything.[1] That means that Jesus came to redeem all things, including our relationships with others, our work, and our life in society. Further, God is working to renew our minds to align with His Kingdom values.

Jesus begins this parable with "The kingdom of heaven is like . . ." (Matthew 20:1), but the disciples in many ways still espoused the values of the world, which are in opposition to the Kingdom of God. This parable is sandwiched between two conversations: Peter's self-congratulatory statement that "we have left everything to follow you! What then will there be for us?" (Matthew 19:27) and John and James's mother asking that her sons sit at Jesus' right and left (Matthew 20:21). She wanted her sons to have places of power and honor in Jesus' Kingdom. When the other ten disciples heard about this, they were indignant.

While the disciples were jockeying for power and seeking glory for themselves, Jesus told them that He would soon die on the cross for them (Matthew 20:18-19). He sought to instill the values of loving servanthood, a hallmark of the Kingdom of God. Those who desire to be great need to learn how to serve—just as Jesus came not to be served "but to serve, and to give his life as a ransom for many" (Matthew 20:28). Jesus is radically others focused and sacrificial in His love.

It is in this context that Jesus told the parable about the laborers in the vineyard. His words give us a window into what God's reign will look like, where generosity is extended to those who have not earned it and the focus is not on getting the most for ourselves but rather on making sure others are provided for and cared for as well (Matthew 19:30; 20:16). Our response to this provocative parable will challenge us to wrestle with our notions of fairness in light of the Kingdom values of grace and generosity.

1. Describe a time someone who did not work as hard as you achieved a better outcome, such as receiving a higher grade in a class, getting a promotion or raise, or beating your team in a sports competition. How did you feel? How did you respond?

____

____

____

____

____

2. Describe a time when you were the recipient of an unexpected act of generosity. How did you feel? How did you respond?

____

____

____

____

____

A denarius was the normal day's pay for manual laborers hired by the day but was barely enough to maintain a family at subsistence level. Often the male day laborer's wife and children "would also have to supplement that income through their own labor and resourcefulness."[3]

"[Day laborers] are dependent on being hired since they do not own their own land. They do not even have the relative security of steady work that slaves have. . . . It is critical that they are hired. If they are not, their family will go hungry."[4]

3. The landowner is not a distant lord but is intimately involved in the harvest, "both in recruiting workers throughout the day and in directing the distribution of wages."[2] How many times does the landowner go out to hire day laborers? And what does he tell each group he will pay them?

____

____

____

____

____

____

____

____

____

4. Some day laborers wait all day to be hired and are still waiting at five o'clock. You would think that they would give up hope and go home before then. Why do you think they are still waiting around?

____

____

____

____

____

____

____

5. At first it appears that the landowner is being frugal by assessing how much work there is to be done before hiring the number of workers he needs. But what is the twist in the parable?

____

____

____

____

____

____

____

____

Precision is important when harvesting in a timely fashion. "If the harvest is a day late, the landowner may lose the crop. But if he is one day too early, the crop may lose value in the marketplace. For the landowner to make the most of his investment, he must hire the appropriate number of workers."[5]

The landowner, whom we may assume is being frugal, is actually shockingly generous. He asks those still waiting around at five o'clock why they are still standing around. He likely hires them out of compassion. They probably won't do that much for him the remaining hour of the day.[6]

6. Usually those who have worked the longest would be paid first, then the next-longest workers would be paid next, and so on. When the laborers who were hired early in the day see that the last ones hired get paid a denarius, they probably expect to be paid more—only to be disappointed when they receive the same payment (even though they agreed to work for that amount)! Why do you think the landowner tells the foreman to reverse the order of payment?

____

____

____

____

____

____

____

____

The landowner wants those who labored all day to see the grace he gives those who have not labored as long.[7] The envy this elicits from the all-day laborers is then contrasted with the generosity of the landowner.

Those who relate to the all-day workers may be upset because the landowner's compassion challenges their sense of justice and fairness. But for those who relate to the eleventh-hour workers, the landowner's generosity is welcome good news and amazing grace.

7. Put yourself in the shoes of a laborer who worked the full day in the hot sun. How would you feel about the way the landowner pays those who have worked less? Now put yourself in the shoes of a laborer who was hired at the last hour. How would you feel about what you are paid?

____

____

____

____

____

____

____

____

____

The full-day workers are treated fairly, since they are paid what they were promised. The landowner reframes the issue as one of generosity. These workers have been so focused on the perceived wrong done to them that they are failing to see that they've been working for a kind and generous employer.[8]

8. What three points does the landowner make to the workers who grumble against him (Matthew 20:13-15)?

____

____

____

____

____

____

____

9. What does the landowner's answer reveal about his character? As you think about God's character (as reflected in the character of the landowner), how does this align with or challenge your view of God?

"The parable instructs us that God's treatment of people, his judgment, is not based on human reckoning and human standards of justice."[9]

____

____

____

____

____

____

____

____

____

10. How can focusing on God's incredibly generous nature change how we understand God's view of others?

"The unexpected twist in the parable should shock us into self-scrutiny; for thus we are betrayed into disclosing our egoism to ourselves. Our stinginess is never more forcibly brought home than when we perceive another's generosity."[10]

"Grace is intended to change us, to make us more like the one who is the primary grace-giver, and the Holy Spirit can open our eyes to see it and our hearts to receive it."[11]

____

____

____

____

____

____

____

____

Your Response

This parable addresses the envy we experience in our hearts when we are offended that God blesses those we consider less faithful or righteous than us. When we compare ourselves to others and think we deserve more, we can become self-righteous. But in reality we are all eleventh-hour workers when it comes to receiving God's grace. We are all poor, sinful, and vulnerable. We have nothing to offer God, yet He has poured out His grace and mercy upon us.

When you accept God's radical generosity to you, you can become more grace filled and generous to others. Your perspective can shift from a scarcity mentality to an abundance mentality, from worrying about what you have to making sure others have enough as well. Consider an area in your life where you may experience envy or have a hard time extending grace to someone. Ask God to help you first receive His grace in a fresh way and then see others through His eyes of grace and generosity.

For Further Study

Read Matthew 19:16-30, which immediately precedes this parable. A young man, a devout Jew who keeps all the commandments, seems to have it all. Luke even refers to him as a "ruler" (Luke 18:18). It is ironic that this rich, law-abiding ruler does not get into the Kingdom while Jesus' "mixed up band of followers from Galilee are promised thrones."[12] Why do you think the young man rejects grace and prefers to justify himself? How is the rich young ruler like those who were hired early in the day in the parable of the laborers in the vineyard? How is he like the Pharisees?

THE GREAT BANQUET

Grace to the Downtrodden (Luke 14:15-24)

DURING SHABBAT (SABBATH) DINNER at the home of a prominent Pharisee, Jesus was being "carefully watched" (Luke 14:1) by those who wanted to see if they could find a theological flaw in His teaching.[1] When a man with edema appeared in front of Him, Jesus asked whether it was lawful to heal on the Sabbath—and then He proceeded to heal the man. He continued to initiate a lively conversation, ranging from refraining from sitting at a place of honor at the table to inviting to dinner those who cannot repay you (Luke 14:1-14).

Then a guest at the table said to Jesus, "Blessed is the one who will eat at the feast in the kingdom of God" (Luke 14:15). A banquet or feast was an image commonly used to describe the day of salvation or the age to come (see Isaiah 25:6; Revelation 19:9). Essentially, the guest's statement meant "Blessed is everyone who is saved."[2] Perhaps the guest presumed that those around the table would inevitably be part of the banquet in the coming Kingdom.

This comment prompted Jesus to launch into the parable of the great banquet, where a master gets increasingly angry as people decline his invitation to come to dinner. The parable challenged the presumption of those present that they would inevitably be attending the feast in the age to come.[3] In the story, the "poor, the crippled, the blind and the lame," and those who live far away end up attending the banquet (Luke 14:21-23). Jesus modeled this in His own table of fellowship, which often included those on the margins: tax collectors, women, sinners, prostitutes, foreigners, and the poor.

New Testament scholar Scot McKnight and pastor Tommy Preson Phillips write,

> Jesus' table gatherings disrupted honor culture and replaced it with love culture. . . . He taught his followers not to judge those at the table with them, as is the pattern of the world. He didn't proclaim their sins, condemn them, or make sure they all agreed with position papers and doctrinal statements. Instead, he filled them up with whatever he had, whether tangible or spiritual.[4]

This parable shows that Jesus' table makes room for all who accept the invitation to come and be loved and forgiven.

---

1. Read Luke 14:15-24. What about the parable resonates with you? What makes you uncomfortable?

____

____

____

____

____

____

____

____

____

____

____

2. Jesus did not dispute the guest's comment in Luke 14:15 that the people who eat at the feast in the Kingdom of God will be blessed. Perhaps the guest was thinking that he and those at the table would enjoy fellowship with God in His coming reign. Do you think he was surprised by Jesus' response? Why or why not?

Metaphorically, the religious leaders at the Shabbat dinner had accepted God's first invitation through their religious observances of the Old Testament. "Now, through Jesus, God was announcing that everything was ready, and his kingdom had arrived. But these very religious men refused to enter the kingdom. They refused to accept, welcome, and follow Jesus. They were, like the guests in the parable, duplicitous in character and insulting to God."[5]

3. The host of the banquet invites numerous people (Luke 14:16). This would be like sending wedding invitations with a request to RSVP. When the banquet is ready, the host sends his servant to tell those who were initially invited that it is time to come (Luke 14:17). Why would it be rude to make excuses at that stage?

---

4. What do you make of the various excuses that the invited guests make in Luke 14:18-20? Are these excuses valid?

____

____

____

____

____

____

____

____

____

5. What do you make of the master's anger in Luke 14:21? Do you think it is justified, or does it surprise you? Why?

____

____

____

____

____

____

____

____

"The striking thing is that 'all' of them declined. 'Alike' (*apo mias*, a unique expression in Greek) does not mean 'in the same way' but probably 'with one accord' or 'all at once.'"[6]

"The excuses vary, but the basic reason is similar, dealing with either financial or familial concerns. Something else is ultimately more important than attending the celebration. Since the eschatological banquet is the object of the allusion, Jesus is making the point that other concerns get in the way of deciding for Jesus and sharing the hope of the eschaton. Such excuses are . . . insulting, in light of the occasion and their previous willingness to come."[7] Ultimately, "no excuse is valid when one faces the kingdom."[8]

"True devotion is not saying 'Yes' to God's invitation, but actually showing up to be with him today. Like the religious leaders of ancient Israel, a person may wish to be seen as devoted to God, but they may not want to submit themselves to life under his reign. That is precisely what happens when we engage in the external forms of religion but reject Jesus' presence and his commandments in our daily lives."[9]

The theme of judgment is also present in Jesus' teaching. "Without the concept of judgment one does not even need salvation, and any urgency about life and its importance, about justice, or even about God is, if not lost, at least greatly diminished. Grace is only grace if the outcome should have been otherwise."[10]

"The inclusion of the maimed is significant in that they were banned from full participation in Jewish worship (Lev. 21:17-23 . . .). The move pictures Jesus' offer of the gospel to the nation's common and needy people."[11]

6. God is generous in extending His invitation to us. Frequently, failure to come is not because of lack of opportunity but perhaps because of lack of willingness to pay the cost of discipleship. Read Luke 9:57-62. What are the similarities in excuses between these three dialogues on discipleship and the parable of the feast?

____

____

____

____

____

____

____

____

7. The host does not reschedule or postpone the feast, because the meal is ready. What does the host ask the servant to do? How does this connect to Jesus' words in the earlier part of the conversation (Luke 14:13)? Why do you think Jesus both led and ended with this focus?

____

____

____

____

____

____

8. Read Isaiah 61:1-3. What strikes you about who receives the good news? How is the news good for those who receive it?

____

____

____

____

____

____

9. The host wants to have a full house for his banquet (Luke 14:22-23). What does this reveal about his heart?

Most commentators hold that the extension of the invitation is the extension of the gospel to the Gentiles.[12]

____

____

____

____

____

10. Where does the host tell the servant to go to issue the third invitation (Luke 14:23)? How do you feel about the host telling his servant to strongly urge the people in those places to come in?

Some translations use the verb _compel_, but the Greek word (_anagkazō_) can have a weakened nuance: "strongly urge" or "invite." "The appeal is not so much to compel people to come in as it is to urge them to attend. . . . Urging is necessary because the people do not know the host and so need encouragement to attend."[13]

____

____

____

____

____

"Holy God, there is always room for one more at your banquet table. We pray to live in such a way that each person we meet knows they are welcome among your people. We welcome you as we welcome others this day. Amen."[14]

11. The invitation to the banquet comes through Jesus and is expansive, reaching people in all directions. There will be people at the table who are poor and needy, and all racial groups will be represented (Revelation 7:9; 19:9). There is no indication that anyone is more or less deserving of being invited. Those who attend the banquet are those who simply accept the invitation and come. What does this reality show you about grace?

Your Response

Review each of the parables of grace in this Bible study. Describe how your view of God's grace has changed or evolved through this study. How does your understanding of grace impact how you relate to God and to others? As we grow in the knowledge of God's grace and love and receive these things personally in our hearts, we are transformed. We cease striving to earn our worth, and we rest in being beloved children of God. We welcome others, we act justly, and we love mercy because we have been the recipients of undeserved grace and are being formed into Christ's likeness. Write a prayer to God, thanking Him for His grace to you, and brainstorm a few practical ways you and your community can practice extending grace to others.

For Further Study

Read Luke 13:22-30. As in the parable of the great banquet, people will come from faraway places and from every direction to participate in the Kingdom of God, and those who are last will be first. Many people assumed that because of their religious heritage, adherence to religious rules or rituals, or proximity to Jesus that they would be saved. Jesus says in John 14:6, "I am the way and the truth and the life. No one comes to the Father except through me." Have you encountered Jesus and accepted His invitation to follow Him? What does entrance to the Kingdom require? Even though the invitation is extended broadly, why is the door considered "narrow" (Luke 13:24)?

NOTES

INTRODUCTION—THE PARABLES OF JESUS

1. Arland J. Hultgren, *The Parables of Jesus: A Commentary* (Grand Rapids: Eerdmans, 2000), 3.
2. Blue Letter Bible, "Lexicon: Strong's G5485—*charis*," accessed June 27, 2024, https://www.blueletterbible.org/lexicon/g5485/kjv/tr/0-1.
3. Ingrid Faro, *Demystifying Evil: A Biblical and Personal Exploration* (Downers Grove, IL: InterVarsity Press, 2023), 192.
4. Philip Yancey, *What's So Amazing about Grace?*, rev. ed. (Grand Rapids: Zondervan, 2023), 46.
5. Faro, *Demystifying Evil*, 193–94.

SESSION ONE—THE SOWER

1. David Wenham, *The Parables of Jesus*, The Jesus Library, ed. Michael Green (Downers Grove, IL: InterVarsity Press, 1989), 42.
2. Michelle Lee-Barnewall, *Surprised by the Parables: Growing in Grace through the Stories of Jesus* (Bellingham, WA: Lexham Press, 2020), 147.
3. As quoted in Craig L. Blomberg, *Interpreting the Parables*, 2nd ed. (Downers Grove, IL: InterVarsity Press, 2012), 21.
4. Wenham, *Parables of Jesus*, 45.
5. Wenham, *Parables of Jesus*, 44.
6. Darrell L. Bock, *Luke: Volume 1 (1:1–9:50)*, Baker Exegetical Commentary on the New Testament (Grand Rapids: Baker, 1994), 739.
7. Bock, *Luke: Volume 1*, 721.
8. Wenham, *Parables of Jesus*, 45.
9. Klyne R. Snodgrass, *Stories with Intent: A Comprehensive Guide to the Parables of Jesus*, 2nd ed. (Grand Rapids: Eerdmans, 2018), 171.
10. Lee-Barnewall, *Surprised by the Parables*, 146.
11. Bock, *Luke: Volume 1*, 728.
12. Bock, *Luke: Volume 1*, 728.
13. Bock, *Luke: Volume 1*, 729.
14. Bock, *Luke: Volume 1*, 729.

15. Bock, *Luke: Volume 1*, 738.

16. Bock, *Luke: Volume 1*, 739.

17. Snodgrass, *Stories with Intent*, 155. "Estimates of normal yields in the ancient world."

18. Michael Card, *Inexpressible: Hesed and the Mystery of God's Lovingkindness* (Downers Grove, IL: InterVarsity Press, 2018), 114.

19. Reuven Kimelman, "The Opening of the Shema Prayer Explained," *The Jewish Experience*, May 2, 2022, https://www.brandeis.edu/jewish-experience/holidays-religious -traditions/2022/may/shema-explained-kimelman.html.

20. Snodgrass, *Stories with Intent*, 8.

21. Skye Jethani, "Abandon the Outcomes," With God Daily, February 7, 2024, https://www .withgoddaily.com/abandon-the-outcomes.

22. Lee-Barnewall, *Surprised by the Parables*, 152–53.

SESSION TWO—THE LOST SHEEP AND THE LOST COIN

1. Kenneth E. Bailey, *The Cross and the Prodigal: Luke 15 through the Eyes of Middle Eastern Peasants*, 2nd ed. (Downers Grove, IL: InterVarsity Press, 2005), 27.

2. Bailey, *The Cross and the Prodigal*, 28.

3. Michelle Lee-Barnewall, *Surprised by the Parables: Growing in Grace through the Stories of Jesus* (Bellingham, WA: Lexham Press, 2020), 13.

4. Michael Chung, "The Redeeming Repast," *Missio Dei: A Journal of Missional Theology and Praxis* (*MDJ*) 7 (Summer–Fall 2016), https://missiodeijournal.com/issues/md-7/authors /md-7-chung.

5. Jeremias, as quoted in Kenneth E. Bailey, *Poet and Peasant*, in *Poet and Peasant* and *Through Peasant Eyes: A Literary-Cultural Approach to the Parables in Luke* (Grand Rapids: Eerdmans, 1983), 142–43. In this work, page numbers start over for *Through Peasant Eyes*. Citations to it specify which title within this book are being referenced.

6. Jeremias, as quoted in Bailey, *Poet and Peasant*, 143.

7. Jeremias, as quoted in Bailey, *Poet and Peasant*, 143.

8. Lee-Barnewall, *Surprised by the Parables*, 14–15.

9. Bailey, *Poet and Peasant*, 147.

10. Klyne R. Snodgrass, *Stories with Intent: A Comprehensive Guide to the Parables of Jesus*, 2nd ed. (Grand Rapids: Eerdmans, 2018), 102.

11. Snodgrass, *Stories with Intent*, 102.

12. Lee-Barnewall, *Surprised by the Parables*, 18.

13. Darrell L. Bock, *Luke: Volume 2 (9:51–24:53)*, Baker Exegetical Commentary on the New Testament (Grand Rapids: Baker, 1996), 1303.

14. Bailey, *The Cross and the Prodigal*, 33.

15. Bock, *Luke: Volume 2*, 1302.

16. Snodgrass, *Stories with Intent*, 109.

17. Amy-Jill Levine, *Short Stories by Jesus: The Enigmatic Parables of a Controversial Rabbi* (New York: HarperOne, 2015), 14.

SESSION THREE—THE PRODIGAL FATHER

1. Michelle Lee-Barnewall, *Surprised by the Parables: Growing in Grace through the Stories of Jesus* (Bellingham, WA: Lexham Press, 2020), 29.

2. Lee-Barnewall, *Surprised by the Parables*, 32.

3. Kenneth E. Bailey, *The Cross and the Prodigal: Luke 15 through the Eyes of Middle Eastern Peasants*, 2nd. ed. (Downers Grove, IL: InterVarsity Press, 2005), 52–53.

4. David Wenham, *The Parables of Jesus*, The Jesus Library, ed. Michael Green (Downers Grove, IL: InterVarsity Press, 1989), 110.

5. Kenneth E. Bailey, *Poet and Peasant*, in *Poet and Peasant* and *Through Peasant Eyes: A Literary-Cultural Approach to the Parables in Luke* (Grand Rapids: Eerdmans, 1983), 196–98.

6. Ingrid Faro, *Demystifying Evil: A Biblical and Personal Exploration* (Downers Grove, IL: InterVarsity Press, 2023), 195–96.

7. Wenham, *Parables of Jesus*, 106.

8. Bailey, *The Cross and the Prodigal*, 43.

9. Walter L. Liefeld and David W. Pao, "Luke," in *The Expositor's Bible Commentary, Volume X: Luke–Acts*, rev. ed., ed. Tremper Longman III and David E. Garland (Grand Rapids: Zondervan, 2010), 253.

10. Bailey, *The Cross and the Prodigal*, 50.

11. Bailey, *Poet and Peasant*, 178.

12. Ann Voskamp, *Waymaker: Finding the Way to the Life You've Always Dreamed Of* (Nashville: W Publishing Group, 2022), 271–72.

13. Bailey, *Poet and Peasant*, 181.

14. Bailey, *Poet and Peasant*, 181–82.

15. Bailey, *Poet and Peasant*, 185.

16. Lee-Barnewall, *Surprised by the Parables*, 31.

17. Bailey, *Poet and Peasant*, 196.

18. Amy-Jill Levine, *Short Stories by Jesus: The Enigmatic Parables of a Controversial Rabbi* (New York: HarperOne, 2015), 73.

19. Klyne R. Snodgrass, *Stories with Intent: A Comprehensive Guide to the Parables of Jesus*, 2nd ed. (Grand Rapids: Eerdmans, 2018), 142.

SESSION FOUR—THE GOOD SAMARITAN

1. Klyne R. Snodgrass, *Stories with Intent: A Comprehensive Guide to the Parables of Jesus*, 2nd ed. (Grand Rapids: Eerdmans, 2018), 353.

2. Michelle Lee-Barnewall, *Surprised by the Parables: Growing in Grace through the Stories of Jesus* (Bellingham, WA: Lexham Press, 2020), 74.

3. David Wenham, The Parables of Jesus, The Jesus Library, ed. Michael Green (Downers Grove, IL: InterVarsity Press, 1989), 159.

4. Don Stewart, "Who Were the Samaritans?" Blue Letter Bible, accessed September 19, 2024, https://www.blueletterbible.org/faq/don_stewart/don_stewart_1319.cfm.

5. New World Encyclopedia, s.v. "Samaritan Pentateuch," accessed November 14, 2024, https://www.newworldencyclopedia.org/entry/Samaritan_Pentateuch.

6. Walter L. Liefeld and David W. Pao, "Luke," in The Expositor's Bible Commentary, Volume X: Luke–Acts, rev. ed., ed. Tremper Longman III and David E. Garland (Grand Rapids: Zondervan, 2010), 199.

7. Snodgrass, *Stories with Intent*, 349–50.

8. Liefeld and Pao, "Luke," 199.

9. Craig S. Keener, *The IVP Bible Background Commentary: New Testament*, 2nd ed. (Downers Grove, IL: InterVarsity Press, 2014), 207–8.

10. Liefeld and Pao, "Luke," 199.

11. Martin Luther King Jr., "I've Been to the Mountaintop," as quoted in "Here Is the Speech Martin Luther King Jr. Gave the Night before He Died," CNN, April 4, 2018, https://www.cnn.com/2018/04/04/us/martin-luther-king-jr-mountaintop-speech-trnd/index.html.

12. Snodgrass, *Stories with Intent*, 358.

13. Lee-Barnewall, *Surprised by the Parables*, 76.

14. Snodgrass, *Stories with Intent*, 347.

15. R. Alan Culpepper, "Luke," in *The New Interpreter's Bible Commentary, Volume IX: Luke, John*, ed. Leander E. Keck (Nashville: Abingdon Press, 1994), 229.

16. Culpepper, "Luke," 230.

17. Snodgrass, *Stories with Intent*, 357.

18. Snodgrass, *Stories with Intent*, 359.

19. Keener, *IVP Bible Background Commentary*, 260.

SESSION FIVE—THE TWO DEBTORS

1. Kenneth E. Bailey, *Through Peasant Eyes*, in *Poet and Peasant* and *Through Peasant Eyes: A Literary-Cultural Approach to the Parables in Luke* (Grand Rapids: Eerdmans, 1983), 3–4.

2. Klyne R. Snodgrass, *Stories with Intent: A Comprehensive Guide to the Parables of Jesus*, 2nd ed. (Grand Rapids: Eerdmans, 2018), 82.

3. Bailey, *Through Peasant Eyes*, 5.

4. Bailey, *Through Peasant Eyes*, 6.

5. Darrell L. Bock, *Luke: Volume 1 (1:1–9:50)*, Baker Exegetical Commentary on the New Testament (Grand Rapids: Baker, 1994), 694.

6. Bock, *Luke: Volume 1*, 695.

7. Bock, *Luke: Volume 1*, 694.

8. Bailey, *Through Peasant Eyes*, 9–10.

9. Bailey, *Through Peasant Eyes*, 9.

10. Bailey, *Through Peasant Eyes*, 8–9.

11. R. Alan Culpepper, "Luke," in *The New Interpreter's Bible Commentary, Volume IX: Luke, John*, ed. Leander E. Keck (Nashville: Abingdon Press, 1994), 170.

12. Snodgrass, *Stories with Intent*, 82.

13. Culpepper, "Luke," 169.

14. Culpepper, "Luke," 171.

15. "Median Weekly Earnings $1,227 for Men, $1,021 for Women, First Quarter 2024," TED: The Economics Daily, US Bureau of Labor Statistics, May 2, 2024, https://www.bls.gov/opub/ted/2024/median-weekly-earnings-1227-for-men-1021-for-women-first-quarter-2024.htm#.

16. Bock, *Luke: Volume 1*, 699.

17. Snodgrass, *Stories with Intent*, 87.

18. Bock, *Luke: Volume 1*, 700.

19. Michelle Lee-Barnewall, *Surprised by the Parables: Growing in Grace through the Stories of Jesus* (Bellingham, WA: Lexham Press, 2020), 68.

20. Bailey, *Through Peasant Eyes*, 21.

21. Carolyn Custis James, "Tamar," in *Vindicating the Vixens: Revisiting Sexualized, Vilified, and Marginalized Women of the Bible*, ed. Sandra Glahn (Grand Rapids: Kregel, 2017), 33.
22. Dieula M. Previlon, *Does God See Me? How God Meets Us in the Center of Our Trauma-Healing Journey* (Colorado Springs: NavPress, 2024), 28.
23. Previlon, *Does God See Me?*, 28.
24. Lee-Barnewall, *Surprised by the Parables*, 65.
25. Bailey, *Through Peasant Eyes*, 18.
26. Snodgrass, *Stories with Intent*, 90.

SESSION SIX—THE PERSISTENT WIDOW

1. Klyne R. Snodgrass, *Stories with Intent: A Comprehensive Guide to the Parables of Jesus*, 2nd ed. (Grand Rapids: Eerdmans, 2018), 453.
2. Snodgrass, *Stories with Intent*, 453.
3. Craig S. Keener, *The IVP Bible Background Commentary: New Testament*, 2nd ed. (Downers Grove, IL: InterVarsity Press, 2014), 161, 227.
4. Kenneth E. Bailey, *Through Peasant Eyes*, in *Poet and Peasant* and *Through Peasant Eyes: A Literary-Cultural Approach to the Parables in Luke* (Grand Rapids: Eerdmans, 1983), 134.
5. Jeremias, as quoted in Bailey, *Through Peasant Eyes*, 133–34.
6. Keener, *IVP Bible Background Commentary*, 227.
7. Darrell L. Bock, *Luke: Volume 2 (9:51–24:53)*, Baker Exegetical Commentary on the New Testament (Grand Rapids: Baker, 1996), 1447.
8. Bailey, *Through Peasant Eyes*, 131–32.
9. R. Alan Culpepper, "Luke," in *The New Interpreter's Bible Commentary, Volume IX: Luke, John*, ed. Leander E. Keck (Nashville: Abingdon Press, 1994), 335.
10. Culpepper, "Luke," 336.
11. Snodgrass, *Stories with Intent*, 461–62.
12. Eugene H. Peterson, *Tell It Slant: A Conversation on the Language of Jesus in His Stories and Prayers* (Grand Rapids: Eerdmans, 2012), 131.
13. Bock, *Luke: Volume 2*, 1451.
14. Bock, *Luke: Volume 2*, 1454–55.
15. Amy-Jill Levine, *Short Stories by Jesus: The Enigmatic Parables of a Controversial Rabbi* (New York: HarperOne, 2015), 242–43.
16. Snodgrass, *Stories with Intent*, 462.
17. Levine, *Short Stories by Jesus*, 243.
18. Bailey, *Through Peasant Eyes*, 136.
19. Frank Stern, as quoted in Craig L. Blomberg, *Interpreting the Parables*, 2nd ed. (Downers Grove, IL: InterVarsity Press, 2012), 369.
20. Evagrius the Solitary, as quoted in Peterson, *Tell It Slant*, 132.
21. Blomberg, *Interpreting the Parables*, 369.
22. Bock, *Luke: Volume 2*, 1456.

SESSION SEVEN—THE LABORERS IN THE VINEYARD

1. David Wenham, *The Parables of Jesus*, The Jesus Library, ed. Michael Green (Downers Grove, IL: InterVarsity Press, 1989), 24–25.

2. Matthew E. Gordley, *Social Justice in the Stories of Jesus: The Ethical Challenge of the Parables* (Hoboken, NJ: John Wiley & Sons Ltd, 2024), 236.
3. Gordley, *Social Justice*, 238.
4. Michelle Lee-Barnewall, *Surprised by the Parables: Growing in Grace through the Stories of Jesus* (Bellingham, WA: Lexham Press, 2020), 44–45.
5. Lee-Barnewall, *Surprised by the Parables*, 45.
6. Wenham, *Parables of Jesus*, 114.
7. Lee-Barnewall, *Surprised by the Parables*, 47.
8. Lee-Barnewall, *Surprised by the Parables*, 49.
9. Klyne R. Snodgrass, *Stories with Intent: A Comprehensive Guide to the Parables of Jesus*, 2nd ed. (Grand Rapids: Eerdmans, 2018), 376.
10. Edward A. Armstrong, *The Gospel Parables* (New York: Sheed and Ward, 1967), 126.
11. Lee-Barnewall, *Surprised by the Parables*, 55.
12. Wenham, *Parables of Jesus*, 115.

SESSION EIGHT—THE GREAT BANQUET

1. Walter L. Liefeld and David W. Pao, "Luke," in *The Expositor's Bible Commentary, Volume X: Luke–Acts*, rev. ed., ed. Tremper Longman III and David E. Garland (Grand Rapids: Zondervan, 2010), 242.
2. Skye Jethani, "A Welcoming Kingdom of Inclusion," With God Daily, February 3, 2023, https://www.withgoddaily.com/a-welcoming-kingdom-of-inclusion.
3. Liefeld and Pao, "Luke," 245.
4. Scot McKnight and Tommy Preson Phillips, *Invisible Jesus: A Book about Leaving the Church and Looking for Christ* (Grand Rapids: Zondervan, 2024), 208.
5. Skye Jethani, "Saying 'Yes' to God's Kingdom Is Not Enough," With God Daily, October 24, 2024, https://www.withGoddaily.com/saying-yes-to-God-isnt-enough.
6. Liefeld and Pao, "Luke," 245.
7. Darrell L. Bock, *Luke: Volume 2 (9:51–24:53)*, Baker Exegetical Commentary on the New Testament (Grand Rapids: Baker, 1996), 1273.
8. Klyne R. Snodgrass, *Stories with Intent: A Comprehensive Guide to the Parables of Jesus*, 2nd ed. (Grand Rapids: Eerdmans, 2018), 313.
9. Jethani, "Saying 'Yes.'"
10. Snodgrass, *Stories with Intent*, 323.
11. Bock, *Luke: Volume 2*, 1276.
12. C. H. Dodd, *The Parables of the Kingdom*, rev. ed. (New York: Scribner, 1961), 94.
13. Bock, *Luke: Volume 2*, 1276-77.
14. Shane Claiborne, Jonathan Wilson-Hartgrove, and Enuma Okoro, *Common Prayer: A Liturgy for Ordinary Radicals* (Grand Rapids: Zondervan, 2010), 407.

Since 1975, NavPress, a business ministry of The Navigators, has been producing books, ministry resources, and *The Message* Bible to help people to know Christ, make Him known, and help others do the same.®

"God doesn't want us to be shy with his gifts, but bold and loving and sensible."
2 Timothy 1:7, *The Message*

Learn more about NavPress:

Learn more about The Navigators:

Find NavPress on social media:

CP2044

LifeChange